The Concise Illustrated Book of
Reptiles

Philip Perry

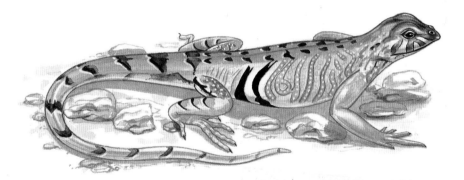

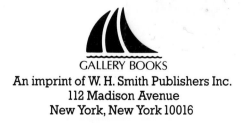

GALLERY BOOKS

An imprint of W. H. Smith Publishers Inc.
112 Madison Avenue
New York, New York 10016

First published in the United States
of America by GALLERY BOOKS
An imprint of W.H. Smith Publishers Inc.
112 Madison Avenue
New York, New York 10016

ISBN 0-8317-1681-9

Printed in Portugal

Acknowledgments
Ardea: Ian Beames 35; Liz and Tony Bomford 34;
J. B. and S. Bottomley 29; Donald D. Burgess 19, 27, 40;
Elizabeth S. Burgess Title page, 4, 26, 38; J. P. Ferrero 32;
Francis Gonier 16; Mazamiro Iijima 10; John Mason 14,
J. L. Mason 13, 21; P. Morris 33, 36, 46; S. Roberts 11;
B. L. Sage 18, 43; Wardene Weisser 28, 41.
J. Allen Cash: 9, 12, 24, 42.
NHPA: 39.
Oxford Scientific Films: Zig Leszcjynski 7, 31;
Stan Osolinski 8.
K. G. Preston-Mafham 20, 22, 23.
Edward Ross 15, 17, 25, 29, 37, 44, 45.

All artworks supplied by Phil Weare/Linden Artists.

Right: Florida Brown Snake

CONTENTS

INTRODUCTION

Many people's instinctive reaction to reptiles, particularly snakes, is one of fear, horror and disgust. Over the centuries they have been greatly misrepresented and the subject of many wildly exaggerated stories. Tales of fierce man-eating dragons and aggressive, vengeful snakes are legion. The truth regarding reptiles is far from their somewhat hysterical treatment in ancient and modern myth. By nature reptiles are not aggressive, although they will defend themselves if they cannot run away. While snakebites can be fatal, they usually are not, and with sensible precautions can be avoided, as humans are only attacked in self-defence. Regrettably snakes' undeserved reputation has led to much indiscriminate killing. Far from being loathsome creatures, reptiles are worth getting to know. They are often very beautiful and are certainly always interesting to observe. As herpetology (the study of reptiles) continues to flourish perhaps the myths will gradually be replaced by at least a tolerant acceptance of this fascinating group of animals.

The reptiles include tortoises, turtles and terrapins, lizards, snakes and crocodiles, and are characterized by their scaly, dry skin. This distinguishes the lizards, for example, from the superficially similar newts, which, being amphibians, have moist skins and no scales. Reptiles are the living descendants of the ancient dinosaurs. The name dinosaur is derived from the Greek words *deinos* and *sauros*, and simply means terrible lizard. In evolutionary terms reptiles are quite primitive animals but some of them evolved into birds, their scales becoming transformed into feathers over the millennia. Other early forms of reptile eventually evolved into the mammals.

Unlike mammals and birds, reptiles are cold-blooded and their body temperature is not maintained at a constant level by the expenditure of metabolic energy. In practice this means that reptiles are the same temperature as their surroundings for much of the time. However, in order to be active, even reptiles must be warm. They can achieve this by basking in the sun, as snakes, lizards and turtles are commonly seen doing. The effect of being cold-blooded is that they have a much slower rate of metabolism than mammals and in consequence do not have to eat as much, as their energy requirements are much less. Thus pythons can survive inactive for several weeks without food and yet lose hardly any weight. In cold climates where the winter temperature falls very low reptiles generally hibernate. They seek refuge in a hole or rock crevice and become virtually dormant so that they do not use up any energy resources. Some turtles even hibernate underwater where they obtain their very meagre oxygen needs directly from the water itself. Nearly all reptiles are carnivorous (meat-eating) though some of the tortoises, all turtles and some lizards are vegetarian, feeding on plants. Different species are active at different times. Many snakes and some lizards come out at night (nocturnal), while most lizards and turtles are active during daytime (diurnal). Others prefer the twilight hours of dawn and dusk (crepuscular). Reptiles are mostly *oviparous*, that is they reproduce by laying eggs. Some, however, are *viviparous*, the eggs developing inside the mother and the young being born alive. In others eggs are laid but hatch almost immediately. Very few reptiles show any signs of parental care for their offspring, but a notable exception is the American alligator. The mother stays with her young for up to two years to protect them, though the young can feed themselves right from birth.

Many reptiles, from terrapins and tortoises to snakes and lizards, are kept as pets. Unfortunately many of them live in very poor conditions. A worrying aspect of the pet trade is that most reptiles sold are caught straight from the wild and the natural populations are now declining, some of them to an alarming extent. Very often many animals die even before they reach the pet stores. If you do intend to keep a reptile as a pet, make sure that it has been bred in captivity. Keep the commoner species rather than the more exotic types as the latter often require very elaborate living conditions and specialized foods otherwise they die.

COOTER

Pseudemys floridana

Family: Emydidae
Distribution: Central, southern and eastern U.S.A. to Florida
Length: 20–40 cm (8–16 in)
Description: The yellow-brown carapace of this basking turtle is relatively unmarked but the head, tail and legs are striped yellow. The plastron (underside) is unmarked or faintly patterned, but there may be irregular dark rings on the underside of the marginal plates (scutes). The young are also yellowish but may be subtly tinged with orange or red. As in all basking turtles the male, which is smaller than the female, has extremely long claws on its forelimbs.

General remarks: Some scientists include this species in the genus *Chrysemys*. The three subspecies are all similar in looks. Preferred habitats are marshes, lakes, ponds and swamps. Though aquatic it spends much time out of the water sunning itself, sometimes with other turtle species, but is very wary. The diet is almost exclusively vegetarian, except when young. One or two clutches of up to 20 eggs are laid in a shallow nest chamber. Each egg is about 3 cm (1 in) long.

FLORIDA SOFTSHELL TURTLE

Trionyx ferox

Family: Trionychidae
Distribution: Florida and southern Alabama to southern South Carolina
Length: Males 15–29 cm (6–11.5 in), females 20–50 cm (8–20 in)
Description: The body is flat and almost circular in shape. The upper shell (carapace) varies from olive when young, to grey or dark brown when adult and has many small raised lumps over its surface. The whitish or grey undershell (plastron) in unmarked. A yellow or red stripe usually runs from jaw to eye. The snout is quite long and somewhat flattened. The tail of the male protrudes well beyond the carapace, in contrast to that of the female which is only just visible from above.

General remarks: The edge of the shell of this freshwater turtle is soft and pliable, hence the name. It is the largest of the North American softshells, preferring still water with a muddy bottom such as lakes, ponds and canals. They are regularly seen sunning themselves on the bank, although more often are buried in mud leaving only nostrils and eyes showing. Powerful swimmers, they feed mainly on small invertebrates such as snails and clams, occasionally fish. The young are much more brightly coloured than the adults. They have large dark irregular rings on the upper shell, rather like a leopard's spots, and the neck and rim of the shell are tinged orange.

GREEN TURTLE

Chelonia mydas

Family: Cheloniidae
Distribution: Tropical seas, occasionally in the temperate seas of North America, especially south California, and more rarely in European waters
Length: 0.7–1.5 m (2.3–5 ft)
Description: Bronze-green when young, it becomes olive or brown when adult, often with dark mottling. The oval shell consists of bony plates over which lie horny plates or scutes. The scutes, which are formed by the outer layer of skin, are the material called tortoiseshell.

General remarks: This marine turtle weighs up to 275 kg (606 lb), though most are nearer 80 kg (176 lb). Unlike most turtles it is, except when young, herbivorous, living almost entirely on marine plants such as sea grass. Some still nest on the sand dunes in parts of Florida, where the females lay 100 to 150 eggs in a hole they dig under cover of darkness. They continue to lay every 12 days or so, laying some 600 eggs in a season, but they only nest every three years. The source of turtle soup, the colour of their fat when cooked gives them their name. The eggs are also eaten and have in the past been collected in their millions, particularly in the Philippines. Hunting has led the species to the brink of extinction, though recent conservation efforts may at last be having some success. Famous for their regular long-distance transoceanic migrations, turtles marked when nesting on Ascension Island have been recovered 2,250 km (1,400 miles) away off the Brazilian coast, where they spend their time when not breeding.

LEATHERBACK TURTLE

Dermochelys coriacea

Family: The only species in the family Dermochelyidae

Distribution: Tropical seas, but it also ranges into the temperate seas of North America and occasionally as far as the coast of Britain. It has also been known to breed in the Mediterranean

Length: 1.2–2.5 m (4–8 ft)

Description: Unusual in having no external shell, the tough, leathery black skin is flecked with white and bears several prominent toothed ridges. In it are embedded many hundreds of small bony plates. The young are covered with small scales that are soon shed.

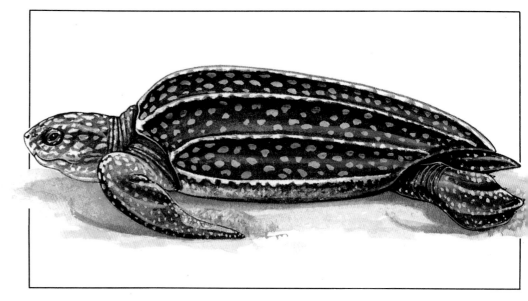

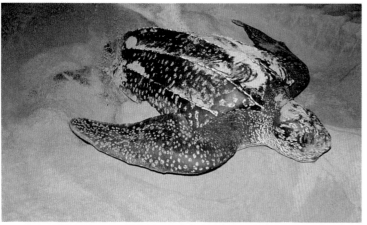

General remarks: This is the largest of all turtles, weighing up to 725 kg (1,600 lb), and is even larger than the giant land tortoises. The adults feed almost entirely on jellyfish, but other foods such as sea urchins, fish and molluscs are sometimes taken. Because of their preference for jellyfish they often risk injury or death by ingesting the similar-looking plastic bags which sadly litter our oceans. Eggs are laid on beaches throughout the tropics, the main nesting areas being French Guiana and Malaysia, though some still nest on the coast of Florida. Each female can lay up to 1,000 eggs in a breeding season, in batches of 100 or so every ten nights. Occasionally referred to by its other name, Luth, it occasionally travels great distances, one individual tagged in South America being recovered 10 months later 6,115 km (3,800 miles) away in West Africa. It is the only strictly pelagic marine turtle as the other species follow the continental shelves. It is an endangered species.

PAINTED TURTLE

Chrysemys picta

Family: Emydidae
Distribution: Eastern and central U.S.A. across to Washington State and southern Canada
Length: 6–25 cm (2–10 in)
Description: A brightly marked fresh-water basking turtle, the flat carapace is nearly black with red markings around the edge. The red lines on the neck become yellow on the head and the legs and tail are also striped red and yellow. The male is quite a lot smaller than the female.

General remarks: Four subspecies are recognized of this most widespread North American turtle, each of which have different markings on the undershell. Often sold as a pet, it is sometimes called the Painted Terrapin. It frequents shallow ponds and marshes with abundant vegetation with still water and a muddy or sandy bottom. It feeds mainly on plants when adult but takes some animals such as snails, crayfish, molluscs and aquatic insects and will also eat carrion. Typically groups are seen basking on logs or the lake bank. They emerge from hibernation around March. There is a particularly elaborate breeding display, in which the male swims backwards in front of the female, stroking her head with the elongated claws of his forefeet. One to four clutches of 2–20 eggs are laid each season.

RED-EARED TERRAPIN

Pseudemys scripta

Family: Emydidae
Distribution: Eastern, central and southern U.S.A., but excluding most of Florida, through to northern Mexico
Length: 9–36 cm (3.5–14 in)
Description: The yellow-brown upper shell (carapace) is variably marked with yellow. Occasionally this colour is masked by black pigment (melanin), and some individuals are completely melanistic. The yellow plastron (underside) generally has a brown mark on each plate. The head, legs and tail all display yellow stripes. The males have long nails on their forefeet.

General remarks: An alternative common name for this terrapin (or turtle according to a few) is Slider, and some authorities classify it in the genus *Chrysemys*. Raised in large numbers on turtle farms they are sold as pets, even as far afield as Britain. The young hatchlings, with shells only 2.5 cm (1 in) across, look very appealing, but unfortunately need very special care and most die after only a short time in captivity. Inhabiting well vegetated lakes, ponds and sluggish rivers, it is often seen sunning itself on logs, but seldom on the bank. It is omnivorous, eating animal and plant matter almost equally. Clutches of 2–25 eggs are laid in late spring or summer. In two of the four subspecies there is a large bright red mark just behind the eye and in another, which is sometimes considered a separate species, the carapace is covered with a pattern of yellow reticulations.

AMERICAN FIVE-LINED SKINK

Eumeces fasciatus

Family: Scincidae
Distribution: Eastern and southern U.S.A., but only northern Florida
Length: Head and body 8.5 cm (3.3 in), tail 13.5 cm (5.3 in)
Description: When young this lizard has a shiny bright blue tail and five pale brown lines or stripes running the length of its dark body. As it matures the tail and body become pale brown to pale grey, with just a few darker marks, thus largely obscuring the lines, though females tend to retain more of the juvenile markings in adult life than males.

General remarks: This skink favours damp places such as log-piles and mounds of rotting vegetation to hide in. Over most of its range it is terrestrial (ground dwelling), but notably in Texas it is arboreal (living mostly in trees). It feeds mostly on insects, spiders, worms and other lizards but on occasion will even eat small mice. In common with many lizards the tail breaks off very easily if handled. This is part of a defence mechanism whereby the brightly coloured cast-off tail, which wriggles as though alive, distracts the predator allowing the skink to escape. Males develop an orange-red colouring to the head during the breeding season. It has opaque eyelids and smooth, rounded scales and unlike many skinks the legs are well developed. Clutches of 4–15 eggs are laid.

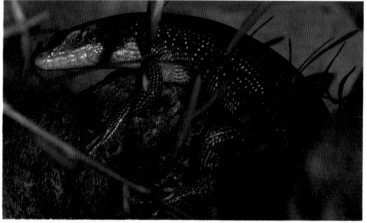

CHUCKWALLA

Sauromalus obesus

Family: Iguanidae
Distribution: Southwestern U.S.A. and Mexico
Length: Head and body 21 cm (8.3 in), tail 20 cm (7.9 in)
Description: Rather flat-bodied with generally small scales, this iguana has distinct loose folds of skin around the neck. Head, body and legs are dark slate grey or blackish with scattered grey and orange flecks. Some individuals have mainly orange or grey bodies with only the head and limbs blackish. The tail, which is very broad at its base and blunt-tipped, is pale yellow. Young lizards have crossbands over the body and a dark-banded tail.

General remarks: Several subspecies are recognized. It is America's largest native iguana and the name derives from the Mexican-Spanish name *chacahuala*. It lives in rocky deserts, particularly those containing the creosote bush, a favourite food. Unusually for a reptile the diet is almost entirely vegetarian, mainly consisting of the leaves, flowers, fruit and buds of desert plants. Diurnal, it is often seen in the late morning or afternoon basking on a rock. If disturbed it will hide in a rock crevice and if threatened further will puff up its body with air, wedging itself so firmly that it cannot be pulled out. Batches of 5–15 eggs are laid towards the end of summer.

COAST HORNED LIZARD

Phrynosoma coronatum

Family: Iguanidae
Distribution: Southwestern U.S.A., south into Mexico
Length: Head and body 10 cm (3.9 in), tail 6 cm (2.4 in)
Description: They may be grey, brown, reddish or yellow. The flattened body is marked with a series of wide transverse dark wavy-edged blotches which extend up to the neck. Large thorn-like scales cover the entire body and tail, and the sides of the body and head are fringed by a double row of spines. The back of the head has a fringe of horns, the two central ones being the longest. The beige or yellow belly is smooth-scaled.

General remarks: Also known as the Horny Toad, this extraordinary looking lizard has a very curious defensive display. It inflates its body with air, opens its mouth and hisses and then jumps towards its would-be attacker in an attempt to bite. If pressed further it will also squirt blood from the corner of its eyes for a distance of about 70 cm (27 in), the significance of which is not really understood. Most of the time it escapes detection by keeping still and relying on its irregular body shape and cryptic coloration. It mostly inhabits open sandy areas though its presence is mainly determined by the availability of the primary food source – ants. Although unfortunately popular as pets the unusual diet makes them particularly unsuitable and most die quickly in captivity. They lay clutches of 6–20 eggs.

DESERT IGUANA

Diposaurus dorsalis

Family: Iguanidae
Distribution: Southwestern U.S.A. and Mexico
Length: Head and body 14 cm (5.5 in), tail 26 cm (10.2 in)
Description: This sizeable, round-bodied lizard, which has very small scales, is pale sand-coloured above with dark red-brown reticulations, and is whitish below. There are many large white spots on the back and sides, some of which are black bordered. The long tail has numerous brown crossbars over its whitish or grey ground colour. A row of keeled scales forms a slightly raised crest down the centre of the back.

General remarks: Of the several subspecies only one occurs in the U.S.A. It inhabits sandy and rocky deserts, living in a burrow. In such arid environments its water requirements are satisfied by a diet of the leaves and flowers of shrubs such as the creosote bush, a particular favourite, and cacti, as well as insects. It can withstand temperatures as high as 45°C (113°F) which would kill most other reptiles and remains active during the heat of the day long after other species have retired underground. The sides of the belly become pink in both males and females in the breeding season. Clutches of 3–8 eggs are laid in summer.

FOX GECKO

Hemidactylus garnoti

Family: Gekkonidae
Distribution: An introduced tropical species found in the U.S.A. only in Miami, Florida and Hawaii. Originally they are from south-east Asia
Length: Head and body 7 cm (2.8 in), tail 6.5 cm (2.6 in)
Description: This gecko is sandy brown and covered by granular scales. The large eyes, which it cleans by licking with its tongue, have vertical pupil slits. The tail has a saw-toothed edge.

General remarks: Also called the Indo-Pacific gecko, it is very vocal and makes a variety of chirping and clicking sounds which may play an important part in defence of its territory. Commonly found in houses, it is active at dusk through the night, feeding on insects. The incredible ability of geckoes to climb up vertical surfaces, and even to hang from a ceiling, is due to the thousands of tiny hooks on the pads of their feet. These hooks are so minute that even on such apparently smooth surfaces as glass they can find irregularities to grip onto. These geckoes are apparently unisexual as no males have been discovered. They reproduce by laying unfertilized eggs in clutches of two in small crevices. Geckoes have been transported along many of the world's shipping lanes both in cargoes and on the ships themselves.

Illustrated, *right*, is a gecko (*Coleonyx variegatus*) of the S.W. desert, Mexico.

GILA MONSTER

Heloderma suspectum

Family: Helodermatidae
Distribution: Southwestern U.S.A. and northern Mexico
Length: Head and body 40 cm (16 in), tail 21 cm (8 in)
Description: The stout, heavy body is covered with bead-like scales, and can be orange, pink or yellow marked with an irregular pattern of black cross-bands. The short, thick tail which has black rings is used to store fat which can be utilized in times of food shortages. The neck skin is loose and hangs in a fold at the throat.

General remarks: Named after the Gila River in Arizona, this is one of only two poisonous lizards in the world, the other being the closely related Beaded Lizard of Mexico. Unlike snakes the venom glands are not in the upper jaw, but in the lower, making the introduction of the neurotoxic venom considerably less efficient as it merely flows into a wound made by biting rather than being injected. The Gila Monster is not aggressive, rarely comes into conflict with humans, and a bite is unlikely to be fatal. It inhabits wooded areas and shrubby deserts and escapes from the heat of the day in a burrow, coming out at night to feed. A favoured food is birds' eggs, but it mainly preys on rodents and other reptiles. A clutch of up to 8 eggs is laid.

GREEN ANOLE

Anolis carolinensis

Family: Iguanidae
Distribution: Southern, central and eastern U.S.A.
Length: Head and body 7.5 cm (3 in), tail 12.5 cm (5 in)
Description: This slender tree-lizard shows a marked difference between the sexes. Males are bright emerald green while females are orange-brown. Males have a large conspicuous bright pink throat fan which can be extended or fully retracted. The males found in Florida tend to be particularly variable in colour and have throat fans that can also be white, magenta or purple.

General remarks: Although it is sometimes called a chameleon, it cannot change colour as quickly as the true chameleons, none of which lives in America. Its colour-change is effected by means of chemical changes in the blood, and so is relatively slow by comparison with true chameleons which use the nervous system. This is the only anole native to the U.S.A., all the other species having been introduced. They climb well and hunt almost entirely by eyesight. Often seen on trees, fences and boardwalks, they feed on insects and spiders. The brightly coloured throat fan is used in territorial and courtship displays, accompanied by vigorous head-bobbing which greatly accentuates it. They lay one egg every two weeks from spring through to autumn.

SAGEBRUSH LIZARD

Sceloporus graciosus

Family: Iguanidae
Distribution: Most of eastern U.S.A. plus small areas in southern and south-western U.S.A. and northern Mexico
Length: Head and body 6.8 cm (2.7 in), tail 8.2 cm (3.2 in)
Description: This spiny lizard, with rough keeled scales on its back, is grey or brown with some dark spots and barring. Two light creamy-brown stripes run lengthwise down the body and are bordered by dark spots that may coalesce to form stripes. There may be a black bar on the shoulder. Males mostly show pale blue mottling on the throat and large dark blue blotches on the sides of the belly while females have orange sides and necks that are particularly noticeable in the breeding season.

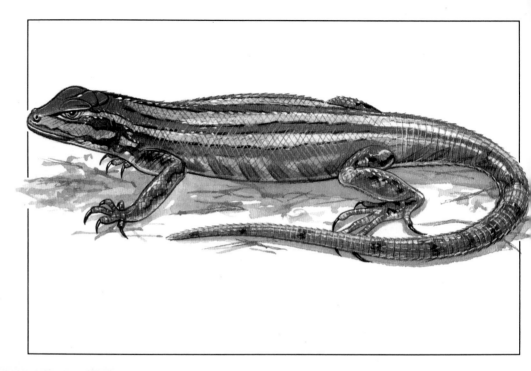

General remarks: Primarily terrestrial, as their name suggests they mostly inhabit areas of sagebrush though they are also found in woodlands, pine forests and brushlands, fleeing to the cover of nearby rocks or thick brush when disturbed. Diurnal, they live on small insects, spiders and other arthropods even including scorpions, and lay batches of 2–8 eggs during the summer.

SAND LIZARD

Lacerta agilis

Family: Lacertidae
Distribution: England and most of Europe, east to Asia as far as Lake Baikal
Length: Head and body 8 cm (3.1 in), tail 12 cm (4.7 in)
Description: A stocky, rather short-legged lizard, the ground-colour tends to be brown, less often green. It normally has a series of broken dark and light stripes along the back. Males have bright green flanks, which intensify in colour when they are breeding. Females are largely brown. Some variants with bright red-brown backs are found in continental Europe. The undersides are white, orange, yellow or green with variable spotting.

General remarks: Unlike the viviparous lizard it is a species of dry habitats such as sandy heaths, hedgerows, field-edges and open woodlands. Unfortunately in Britain habitat destruction has led to a decline in numbers though its status as a protected species is beginning to show positive effects. Although not a montane species it may be found at altitudes of 2,000 m (6,500 ft). They often live in colonies and may hibernate in groups. Omnivorous, their food mostly consists of insects and spiders and in turn they are extensively preyed upon by Smooth Snakes. Six to twelve eggs are laid in a shallow hole dug by the mother.

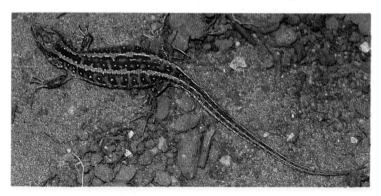

SLOW-WORM

Anguis fragilis

Family: Anguidae
Distribution: Britain and Europe east to Asia Minor and parts of north-west Africa
Length: Up to 50 cm (1.6 ft)
Description: Males are relatively uniformly coloured, either brown, grey, reddish or even coppery and sometimes have small blue spots irregularly over the sides. The brown females tend to have a dark vertebral stripe and dark sides. The very smooth scales give the Slow-worm a highly polished look. The young are metallic gold or silver with a dark vertebral stripe and sides.

General remarks: Although it looks superficially snake-like the Slow-worm is actually a legless lizard of which several subspecies have been described. It is found in a variety of habitats but prefers thick vegetation. Rather secretive, it spends a lot of time in a burrow or under stones or logs but is regularly seen in the early evening especially just after rain. It eats various invertebrates such as insects, slugs, spiders and earthworms, and is preyed upon by many birds and mammals as well as other reptiles such as vipers. In the breeding season, the males fight fiercely for a mate, seizing each other by the head and sometimes inflicting quite severe wounds. The 6–12 young are live-born. It is a long-lived lizard, one captive specimen having reached 54 years.

TREE LIZARD

Urosaurus ornatus

Family: Iguanidae
Distribution: Central southern U.S.A. and northern Mexico
Length: Head and body 6 cm (2.4 in), tail 10 cm (3.9 in)
Description: This small lizard is light brown or grey with an irregular mosaic of dark brown markings forming a cryptic pattern that perfectly conceals it against the bark of a tree trunk. It has a fold of skin across the throat as well as long folds along the sides of the body which give a rather puckered appearance. There are two rows of enlarged keeled scales down the middle of the back.

General remarks: Diurnal, they inhabit trees, rocks and buildings in arid areas up to 2,750 m (9,020 ft). Many subspecies have been described which have slight differences in markings. Males have bright blue or blue-green patches on both the belly and on the yellow or orange throat. Females lack these blue patches but do have the yellow or orange coloured throat. The ear openings are quite noticeable. Black phases are sometimes seen. The excellent camouflage means they are often only seen when they make the characteristic bobbing movements. Prey includes spiders, insects and other small arthropods and they lay clutches of 3–13 eggs.

VIVIPAROUS LIZARD

Lacerta vivipara

Family: Lacertidae
Distribution: Native to Britain, it is also found in most of Europe and northern Asia across to the Mongolian coast
Length: Head and body 6.5 m (2.6 in), tail 10 cm (3.9 in)
Description: Short-legged, with a rounded head, the ground colour is quite variable but mostly brown or olive. There are a number of pale and dark spots (ocelli), which in females often merge into irregular dark stripes. The throat is whitish and the belly can be white, yellow, orange or red.

General remarks: Alternatively called Common Lizard, this species lives as far north as the Arctic circle, the only lizard to do so. Not a lover of very high temperatures, in the southern part of its range it lives in cooler mountainous regions at altitudes up to 3,000 m (10,000 ft). It is generally a ground-dweller, preferring damp areas, and lives in a wide range of habitats from hedgerows, heaths, and woods to sand dunes. It swims adeptly and will, on occasion, hunt for food in the water. Its sense of hearing is good and is put to use when hunting insects and spiders. In winter it hibernates to escape the severe cold and relative lack of food. As the name (viviparous) suggests, the 5–8 young are born live.

WESTERN FENCE LIZARD

Sceloporus occidentalis

Family: Iguanidae
Distribution: Western U.S.A. south into Mexico
Length: Head and body 9.5 cm (3.7 in), tail 14 cm (5.5 in)
Description: Variable in colour, this spiny lizard is generally black or brown with a series of broad, wavy lateral spots across the back. Males have very bright blue throat patches and sides to the belly and also green or blue spots scattered over the back. Females lack blue or green markings above and are much duller underneath. The body and tail are armoured with spiny scales. The backs of the legs are yellow or orange.

General remarks: Colloquially known as Blue-belly or Swift Lizards, they are characteristically seen basking in the sun atop a fence post. There are six subspecies which differ slightly in anatomy and colour. They occupy a variety of habitats from chaparral, sagebrush and grassland to coniferous forest and woodland. These terrestrial carnivorous lizards prey on insects and other arthropods. The males display their bright blue patches during mating displays, which include much head bobbing. Up to three clutches of 3–17 eggs are laid in spring or summer.

BROWN SNAKE

Storeria dekayi

Family: Colubridae
Distribution: The eastern half of the U.S.A. and around the Great Lakes in Canada
Length: 23–48 cm (9–19 in)
Description: The overall colour can be pale sandy brown, red brown or dark brown. There are two rows of dark brown or black blotches across the back, a large dark streak at the corner of the mouth and a dark half-collar at the back of the neck. The scales are keeled.

General remarks: The Latin name honours the well-known New York naturalist, James Edward DeKay. There are five sub-species in the U.S.A. which differ slightly from each other in details of patterning and coloration. The subspecies known as the Florida Brown Snake has only 15 rows of scales as opposed to 17 in all the others. Quite common in urban areas, though much less so than formerly, they are also found in swamps, marshes and boggy habitats. These small snakes feed primarily on earthworms, slugs and insects. Three to thirty young are born in summer or autumn.

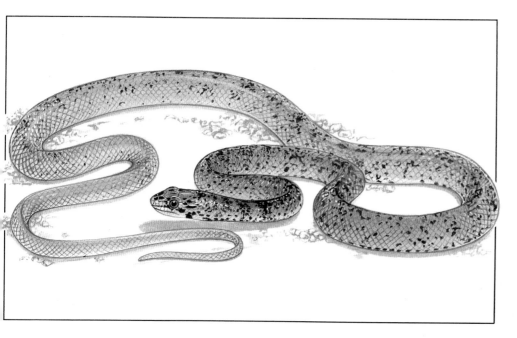

COACHWHIP

Masticophis flagellum

Family: Colubridae
Distribution: Widespread over the southern half of the U.S.A. and southwards into Mexico
Length: 1–1.5 m (3.3–4.9 ft). The record length is 2.6 m (8.5 ft)
Description: The seven subspecies of this slender, long-tailed snake differ widely in appearance. The base colour can be brown, yellow, pink, red, grey or even black. The belly colour is the same as that of the back. Most have no pattern though some do have thick black bars on the neck and others have black zigzags down the body. The tail often has a dark–light pattern reminiscent of the braiding of a whip, hence the name.

General remarks: Much famed for its rapidity, this has been greatly exaggerated and it probably cannot keep up a speed faster than 4 or 6 km per hour (3 or 4 mph). Nevertheless it is America's quickest snake and when threatened vibrates its tail and is quick to strike even though it is not poisonous. They prefer dry open country such as prairies and desert scrub up to 2,130 m (7,000 ft) and in some parts are known as Prairie Runners. Active during the day they feed on other snakes including rattlesnakes, lizards, small mammals, frogs and large insects such as grasshoppers. The clutches of 4–16 eggs are covered in small nodules which give them a rough feel.

COMMON GARTER SNAKE

Thamnophis sirtalis

Family: Colubridae
Distribution: Southern Canada and the U.S.A., south to Costa Rica
Length: 46 cm–1.3 m (1.5–4.3 ft)
Description: These slender snakes vary enormously in colour from one subspecies to another. One is red with vivid black and yellow stripes and black bars. Another is whitish with red, black and yellowish stripes. Yet another is brown with yellow, black and white stripes.

General remarks: Garter snakes are among the most numerous and widely distributed American snakes and reach the most northerly latitudes of all American reptiles. Twelve subspecies occur in discrete areas across the country. Their name comes from the similarity of their longitudinal striping to the patterns on garters which used to be worn by gentlemen to support their socks. They are often quite social and large numbers may hibernate together. Disliking intense heat they prefer moist habitats and frequently swim, and may be found in marshes, woods and prairies from sea level to mountain slopes. Non-venomous, they prey chiefly on frogs, salamanders, small rodents and earthworms and will also eat carrion. The young are born live in broods of 25 or more.

COMMON KING SNAKE

Lampropeltis getulus

Family: Colubridae
Distribution: Most parts of southern U.S.A. and Mexico
Length: 75 cm–2.1 m (2.4–6.9 ft)
Description: This black or dark brown snake is variably patterned with white or yellowish markings that usually take the form of crossbands or broad stripes. Some individuals are speckled while others are dark without any bands. The belly colour is also variable, from white to black. The scales are smooth, not keeled.

General remarks: Seven subspecies are found in the U.S.A., frequenting many habitats from coniferous forest and broadleaved woodland to marshes and deserts, and can be looked for in rocky outcrops and under decaying logs. Though generally terrestrial they swim well. They are notorious for their practice of feeding on other snakes, many of which are poisonous, even including the potentially deadly rattlesnakes, copperheads and coral snakes. This habit has afforded them a good degree of protection from human persecution. Non-venomous, they kill their prey by constriction and may have a measure of immunity from the venom of other snakes. They also catch small mammals, lizards and turtles. Largely diurnal, they will also come out at night, especially in hot weather. Clutches of 2–24 eggs are laid in the summer.

COMMON WATER SNAKE

Natrix sipedon

Family: Colubridae
Distribution: Eastern U.S.A. and south-eastern Canada
Length: 56 cm–1.3 m (1.8–4.3 ft)
Description: This species has a bewildering array of colour varieties. The basic colour varies from dark brown to pale grey. The markings, which mostly consist of broad crossbands, are usually reddish or black. Some individuals are blotched, rather than banded, towards the tail. The underbelly pattern is made up of regular half-moon shapes on a ground of yellow or orange. The markings are most distinct when young and on some adults may fade completely.

General remarks: There are four subspecies of this snake, which is the American counterpart of the European Grass Snake and is sometimes classified in the genus *Nerodia*. They live in swamps, marshes and all other moist environments, though preferably still or slow flowing. Occasionally they are also found by fast-moving rivers and even waterfalls. As their name suggests they are competent swimmers and catch most of their prey in the water. Though harmless, their resemblance to the poisonous Cottonmouth has led to many being needlessly killed. Their food consists of salamanders, frogs and fish. Commonly sunning themselves on logs in the water, they quickly take fright if disturbed and swim away. Fifteen to thirty young are live-born at the end of summer or autumn. Illustrated, *left*, is the Brown Water Snake, *Natrix taxi spilota*.

CORN SNAKE

Elaphe guttata

Family: Colubridae
Distribution: Central, southern and eastern U.S.A. and eastern Mexico
Length: 60 cm–1.8 m (2–5.9 ft)
Description: The subspecies are very different indeed, ground colour varying from orange through yellow to grey or tan. Over this is an irregular mosaic of blackish, reddish or brown blotches. The belly is chequered black on white and the underside of the tail is striped black.

General remarks: Their name probably refers to the resemblance of the belly markings to the pattern of corn kernels on a cob. They have been known to live for 21 years in captivity. Living in a wide range of habitats, including woods, coniferous forests, farmland and near streams, they are often found in rock outcrops and under logs. They climb well, but are more often found on the ground, and they also burrow. When cornered they rear up and open their mouth, threatening to strike, and vibrate their tail. Mostly nocturnal, they feed particularly on small rodents but also take lizards and birds, which are killed by constriction. Because of this food preference they, along with the other species in the genus, are collectively known as rat snakes. Clutches of 3–20 eggs are laid in summer.

COTTONMOUTH

Agkistrodon piscivorus

Family: Viperidae
Distribution: Southern and southeastern U.S.A.
Length: 80 cm–1.9 m (2.6–6.2 ft)
Description: A large dark brown or olive snake with broad, light-bordered cross-bands. The head may be distinctly marked with horizontal whitish bands. All these markings may fade somewhat with age. The young are more brightly coloured and have a yellow tip to the tail.

General remarks: Its name refers to the inside of the mouth which is conspicuously white, and can be seen quite clearly when it is opened wide in defensive or aggressive displays. Alternatively known as Water Moccasin or Trap Jaw it lives mostly in swamplands and lakesides. Some resemble the non-venomous water snakes and can be difficult to tell apart in the field. However the shy water snakes are more likely to swim away quickly when disturbed, whereas the Cottonmouth may move off slowly, or if cornered adopt a defensive posture. Their food consists of fish, frogs, turtles and very young alligators, which are killed with their powerful venom. They have been known to live more than 20 years in captivity. About eight young are born live during early September.

EASTERN DIAMONDBACK RATTLESNAKE

Crotalus adamanteus

Family: Viperidae
Distribution: Southeastern U.S.A., including Florida, within 160 km (100 miles) of the coast
Length: 80 cm–2.4 m (2.6–7.9 ft)
Description: The basic colour is pale sandy brown or olive, occasionally almost black. Down the centre of the back are the famous brown diamond-shaped markings outlined in yellow or cream that gives this snake its name. The tail has black rings and a black tip. There is a dark smudge between the eye and the mouth.

General remarks: This is America's largest poisonous snake. It can be dangerous because it allows a much nearer approach before giving a warning rattle than the closely related Western Diamondback, but only attacks if threatened. Unfortunately their reputation has led to considerable senseless and unjustified slaughter by hunters. This is one of the many species of mailed rattlesnakes, which can be identified by the few large and many small scales on the top of the head, the latter resembling the chain mail of olden times. They inhabit brush country and dry pinelands rather than marshy areas although they swim competently. They catch rabbits as well as other small mammals and birds. The ten or so young measure about 30 cm (1 ft) when born.

EUROPEAN ADDER

Vipera berus

Family: Viperidae
Distribution: Britain and Europe east to the Pacific coast of the U.S.S.R.
Length: Up to 65 cm (2.1 ft), rarely to 90 cm (3 ft)
Description: The most frequent pattern consists of a dark zigzag vertebral stripe over a base colour of grey or brown, with dark spots along the sides. The top of the head is dark and the belly is usually grey or brownish. The tip of the tail can be yellow, orange or red. Other colour variants occur in different parts of its range.

General remarks: Also called the Common Viper, it is Britain's only poisonous snake and although its venom is not particularly potent it can be dangerous to children. It can survive quite cold climates and lives at altitudes up to 3,000 m (10,000 ft). It is the only snake found inside the Arctic circle and like the only other reptile which lives there, the Viviparous Lizard, gives birth to live young, an adaptation suited to the Arctic climate as it allows the mother to keep the young warm until they are born. Occupying a wide range of habitats, from moorland and bogs to open woods and meadows, it enjoys sunning itself and has favoured basking sites. Primarily diurnal and crepuscular, it feeds on small rodents such as voles, slow-worms and lizards. After striking the prey and injecting it with venom, the adder waits for this to take effect. This is usually very quick but sometimes the animal may run away, forcing the snake to track it by scent before the victim finally succumbs to the toxins.

GRASS SNAKE

Natrix natrix

Family: Colubridae
Distribution: England, Wales and the rest of Europe eastwards to central Asia and also North Africa
Length: Normally up to 1.2 m (3.9 ft), but can be as long as 2 m (6.6 ft)
Description: Numerous colour variations exist in different regions. The character common to most is a yellow collar bordered in black just behind the head, though even this is sometimes white or orange. The basic ground colour is olive-green with various degrees of black barring or spotting.

General remarks: Also referred to as the Ringed Snake, it favours moist areas such as damp woodlands, riversides and marshes. Often found in water hunting one of its favourite foods, the Common Frog, it also eats toads, small mammals and even fish. Non-venomous, after seizing its prey in its jaws it simply proceeds to swallow it head first. If threatened it sometimes lies on its back with its mouth open and tongue projecting, feigning death to discourage attack. The species is unusual in that it seeks out places in which heat is generated, namely rotting vegetation, to lay its batches of about 30 or 40 eggs. Different females often lay eggs in the same place resulting in 'plagues' of hundreds of young grass snakes.

INDIGO SNAKE

Drymarchon corais

Family: Colubridae
Distribution: Two discrete populations, one in southeastern Georgia and Florida and the other in Texas and Mexico. Other subspecies and races occur south to Brazil and Argentina
Length: 1.5–2.9 m (4.9–9.5 ft)
Description: Two subspecies are found in the U.S.A. The eastern one is uniformly deep blue-black apart from a reddish or orange-brown area below the eye. The Texas subspecies is more brownish with a vague pattern on the front of the body and also has a reddish belly and several small dark lines leading down from the eye. The scales are glossy in appearance.

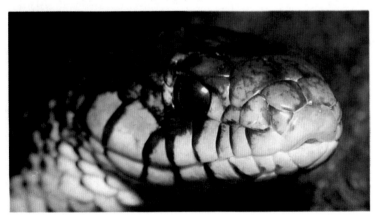

General remarks: The longest snake in the U.S.A., this is a protected species. Because of its habit of sharing a burrow with the Gopher Tortoise it is sometimes called a Gopher Snake, though there is a different species altogether that is more usually referred to by this name. Non-venomous, its prey however includes poisonous snakes such as rattlesnakes and cottonmouths. It also eats small mammals, frogs and birds. When threatened it hisses, vibrates its tail and flattens its neck vertically. Clutches of 5–12 eggs are laid in spring or early summer.

MASSASAUGA

Sistrurus catenatus

Family: Viperidae
Distribution: Parts of southern and central U.S.A. and around the Great Lakes in Canada
Length: 40 cm–1 m (1.3–3.3 ft)
Description: This heavy-bodied, pale creamy-brown or dark grey snake has a series of very broad, somewhat rounded, dark brown or grey bands across its back in a ladder pattern. It also has dark brown spots along the sides and a long dark brown eyestripe as well as diagnostic dark streaks on the top of the head. This species is one of the plated rattlesnakes, which are characterized by nine large scales (plates) on the top of the head.

General remarks: Like all other rattlesnakes the Massasauga is highly venomous and belongs to the group called pit vipers. This name refers to the heat-sensitive organ situated in a pit between the eyes and nostrils, and which is used to track warm-blooded animals at night by sensing the infrared radiation (heat) emitted. Massasaugua means 'great river mouth' in the language of the Chippewa Indians. Sometimes known as Swamp Rattlers they are generally denizens of swamplands, bogs and moist prairies but are also found in dry woodlands and plains. They live on small mammals, snakes and frogs, and are often seen at harvest time when they seek out mice in sheaves of wheat. They produce between 2–19 live young in late summer or autumn.

RED-BELLIED SNAKE

Storeria occipitomaculata

Family: Colubridae
Distribution: Most of the eastern half of the U.S.A. and southeastern Canada
Length: 20–41 cm (8–16 in)
Description: The general colour of this small snake varies from grey to brown, occasionally black, while the top of the head is usually blackish. A buff, black-bordered stripe or four narrow dark stripes run down the centre of the back. Just behind the head are three large buffy spots which may be fused into a continuous collar. As the name indicates, the belly is bright red, though it may sometimes be orange or pale yellow. The scales are keeled.

General remarks: There are three subspecies which show slight differences in the amount of spotting and the form of the nape collar. They inhabit sphagnum bogs, wooded uplands and mountains, and can often be found in clearings or near buildings and outhouses up to 1,700 m (5,580 ft). Rather secretive by nature, they mostly eat slugs, insects and earthworms. They are live bearers, and produce 1–21 young in summer or autumn.

ROSY BOA

Lichanura trivirgata

Family: Boidae
Distribution: Southwestern U.S.A.
Length: 60–110 cm (2–3.6 ft)
Description: This shiny, smooth-scaled, heavy-bodied snake has quite small eyes with vertical pupil slits. Colour is variable, rosy-red, grey or sandy brown, with three brown or grey stripes or series of blotches running the length of the body. The creamy undersides are spotted brown or grey. The scales on the top of the head, which is only just wider than the neck, are small in contrast with those of the Rubber Boa.

General remarks: Favoured habitats are arid areas of scrub and brush that nevertheless have water sources such as a spring or occasional river. They are found at altitudes up to about 1,350 m (4,430 ft). Though good at climbing they are mostly terrestrial and hunt at dusk or at night for small mammals, birds and lizards which they kill by constriction. Males have two spurs on their undersides which are used to stimulate females during courtship. Three to ten young are live-born in the autumn.

ROUGH GREEN SNAKE

Opheodrys aestivus

Family: Colubridae
Distribution: Eastern and southeastern U.S.A. and Mexico
Length: 20 cm–1.2 m (8 in–3.9 ft)
Description: Bright green above, and white, yellow or pale green beneath, it is uniformly coloured with no markings. It is a delicate, slender snake with quite large eyes and a tapering tail. Unlike the closely related Smooth Green Snake, this species has rough, keeled scales.

General remarks: They inhabit areas such as lake margins with thick vegetation at altitudes up to 1,500 m (4,920 ft). Most of the time these placid snakes are arboreal and can be nearly invisible when resting among the vines they so closely resemble. They swim well and quite often. Mostly diurnal, they rely primarily on excellent eyesight when hunting. Non-venomous, they prey on crickets, grasshoppers, spiders, and insect larvae. The colour fades to bluish very quickly after death, and corpses can be difficult to identify. Batches of 3–12 eggs are laid in summer.

RUBBER BOA

Charina bottae

Family: Boidae
Distribution: Northwest U.S.A. and southwestern Canada
Length: 35 cm–1 m (1–3.3 ft)
Description: Stout bodied, it is uniformly olive, brown or grey above, yellowish beneath. Occasional small grey flecks on the sides are the only markings. The top of the head is crowned with large symmetrical scales and the very small eyes have vertical pupils.

General remarks: The prehensile tail and the head are similarly shaped and if the snake is threatened the tail is raised and waved back and forth. Reminiscent of a snake about to strike, this often frightens away potential predators, so protecting the head which is kept hidden within its coils. It is the most northerly boa, all the other species preferring the more tropical climate of Central and South America. It inhabits a wide range of habitats from coniferous or deciduous forest to grasslands. It spends much time burrowing, hence the rather flattened shape of the head. Feeding on shrews or mice as well as other reptiles such as lizards and snakes, it kills its prey by constriction. Between one and eight live young are produced in the autumn.

SMOOTH SNAKE

Coronella austriaca

Family: Colubridae
Distribution: Southern England and Europe and east to the Caucasus
Length: 60–80 cm (2–2.6 ft)
Description: Generally grey or browish, there is a regular pattern of small or· large dark spots along the back and sometimes down the sides. A dark line runs from the jawline through to the nostril. The belly is uniformly dark but varies from red to blackish. At first glance this snake resembles an adder but on closer inspection the head is smaller, the tail longer and the body narrower.

General remarks: This is Britain's rarest snake, being confined to a relatively few localities in the south. A favourite food, in Britain, is the Sand Lizard, but on the continent they also eat Wall and Green Lizards. In addition they catch small mammals and young snakes such as vipers. Non-venomous, when they have caught their prey several coils are wrapped around it to prevent it struggling and it is then swallowed. There are reports that they kill by constriction, as do the boas, but this is probably quite rare. Their preference is for dry habitats such as heaths and open woods, although they will drink readily. The young are born live in broods of 2–15.

TIMBER RATTLESNAKE

Crotalus horridus

Family: Viperidae
Distribution: Central and eastern U.S.A., excluding Florida
Length: 90 cm–1.9 m (3–6.2 ft)
Description: This snake has several colour phases, and may be sandy brown, yellowish or very dark brown. Large black or dark brown blotches form wide bands cross the back and sides. A subspecies, the Canebrake, has a reddish stripe down the centre of the front part of the back as well as a wide dark streak leading from the eye.

General remarks: Like all rattlesnakes, when alarmed it coils itself into a circle, raises the tail rattle in the centre and threatens with the open mouth, exposing long fangs. Because of their length, the fangs are very efficient at delivering a large dose of poison, which is one of the main reasons a rattlesnake bite is so dangerous. Such defensive displays are accompanied, of course, by the famous rattling. Sometimes called Banded or Velvet-tail Rattler, it lives in rocky, timber-covered habitats from the lowlands to mountains, and is America's commonest rattlesnake. It feeds mainly on small rodents such as mice, but also takes squirrels and rabbits. They often hibernate communally and hundreds have been seen together at one site. Five to seventeen young are live-born in late summer or autumn.

WESTERN DIAMONDBACK RATTLESNAKE

Crotalus atrox

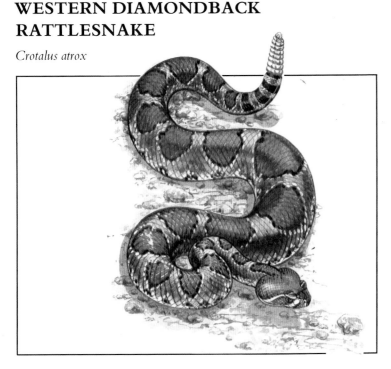

Family: Viperidae
Distribution: Southern U.S.A. and northern Mexico, with an isolated population in southern Mexico
Length: 80 cm–2.1 m (2.6–6.9 ft)
Description: More grey-brown than the eastern species, it also has the dark brown diamond pattern on the back, edged in white but much less strongly marked. The tail is paler than the rest of the body and has black and white rings, hence the vernacular name Coontail. Wide dark and yellow streaks run between eye and mouth. Patterning on the young is more noticeable.

General remarks: The rattle consists of interlocking horny plates which, when vibrated at high speed, cause the well-known rattling sound that the snake uses to deter potentially dangerous intruders. Each time the snake moults another rattle segment is added, but as parts often break off very large rattles are quite rare. These rattlesnakes live in the prairies and arid areas up to 1,500 m (5,000 ft), where they hunt rabbits, ground squirrels and birds. When threatened they are quite aggressive, and since they are fairly common, they are one of the most frequent agents of snakebite in the U.S.A. Nevertheless, like all snakes, they only strike at man in order to defend themselves. Despite this they have increasingly become the target of appallingly cruel treatment in so-called 'rattler round-ups' which annually claim the lives of hundreds of thousands of rattlesnakes. Four to twenty-five young are born in spring or early summer.

AMERICAN ALLIGATOR

Alligator mississippiensis

General remarks: A relatively noisy reptile it produces a range of grunts and bellows. It eats garfish, turtles and waterbirds. Often the swamps and bayous which it inhabits partially dry up and in order to survive it digs out a deep hole which holds water throughout the dry season. These 'gator holes' are very important ecologically and become vital refuges for vast numbers of fish and birds that in turn attract predators such as herons, otters and bobcats. At one time this alligator was severely threatened by hunting for its hide, but protection measures in recent years have led to a good recovery in the population, though in parts it is still endangered. Now farmed for tourism and for their hides, some have lived in captivity for more than 50 years, making it one of the longest lived reptiles. The female guards her nest of 20–50 eggs from predation by skunks and raccoons during the 65-day incubation period. When the young are about to hatch, they emit a loud squeaking which stimulates the mother to help dig them out. Though they can feed themselves, she stays with them for about a year to protect them from predators. This degree of parental care is very unusual, for most reptiles take no part in raising their young.

Family: Alligatoridae
Distribution: Southeastern U.S.A.
Length: 2–5 m (6.6–16.4 ft) on average, the record specimen measuring 5.8 m (19 ft)
Description: Black in colour, it has a blunt rounded snout. When young it is striped with yellow crossbands.

AMERICAN CROCODILE

Crocodylus acutus

Family: Crocodylidae
Distribution: Southern Florida in the U.S.A., and also the West Indies, Central America and northwestern South America
Length: One of the largest crocodile species, it averages 2–4 m (6.6–13 ft) but exceptionally reaches 4.6 m (15 ft) in the U.S.A. In South America it grows to 7 m (23 ft)
Description: It has a somewhat pointed head and a long snout. Smaller adults are olive brown, older ones dull grey. The fourth tooth on the lower jaw can always be seen, even when the mouth is closed when it rests in a notch in the upper jaw, helping to distinguish it from an alligator.

General remarks: This species inhabits brackish swamps and salt-water areas. The raised nostrils allow it to breathe while the body is kept submerged. It swims by powerful movements of the laterally flexible tail. Often seen with its cavernous mouth gaping wide open, this probably helps it to cool down due to evaporation from the mouth lining. Surprisingly its presence in Florida, where it is restricted to the southern tip of the Everglades National Park and the Florida Keys, was only discovered as late as 1875. It is quite rare throughout its range and at one time the numbers in Florida were down to fewer than 500 individuals. Among the fish it catches are bass, tarpon and mullet. A nest is scraped out of mud for the 35–50 eggs. The young are green with thin black crossbands or spots

GLOSSARY

Arthropod: Any of numerous invertebrates having a segmented body and jointed limbs.

Carapace: A hard, bony outer covering. The upper surface of a turtle or tortoise shell.

Crepuscular: Becoming active at dusk or dawn.

Diurnal: Active during the day.

Herpetology: The study of reptiles and amphibians.

Keeled scale: A scale having a longitudinal ridge like a ship's keel.

Nocturnal: Active during the night.

Ocelli: Round eye-like spots.

Oviparous: Reproducing by laying eggs.

Pelagic: Living in open oceans or seas.

Plastron: The under surface of a turtle or tortoise shell.

Reticulation: A network.

Scute: An enlarged scale or plate, as on a turtle shell.

Viviparous: Giving birth to live offspring that develop inside the mother's body.